Me, Myself and I
All about sex and puberty

written by Louise Spilsbury

illustrated by Mike Gordon

BARRON'S

First edition for the United States and Canada
published in 2010 by Barron's Educational Series, Inc.

First published in 2009 by Wayland, a division
of Hachette Children's Books,
an Hachette UK company

All inquiries should be addressed to:
Barron's Educational Series, Inc.
250 Wireless Boulevard
Hauppauge, New York 11788
www.barronseduc.com

ISBN-13: 978-0-7641-4508-7
ISBN-10: 0-7641-4508-8

Library of Congress Control No.: 2009938891

Printed in China
9 8 7 6 5 4 3 2 1

About this book

There are two types of helpful boxes in this book:

Top Tips

These offer useful advice. Some are just for boys; they are blue. Some are just for girls; they are pink. The purple boxes are for both!

Check It Out

These offer snippets of useful information.

There are quizzes at the end of most chapters. The answers can be found on page 61.

Contents

This is puberty!

You have been changing since the day you were born, but since the age of two, the changes have been gradual and mainly involved you growing taller. Now you are probably finding that there are more changes to deal with, and some of them are happening surprisingly quickly. Your body is starting to alter in many ways, inside and out, and you're changing physically and emotionally. This is puberty, the part of your life when you grow from a child into an adult.

Why do you need to know all this?

If puberty is something that just happens, why do you need to read about it? For one, it makes sense to know what is going on with your body so that you can be prepared. Finding out more about puberty will also help you deal with the practical side of it, from shaving to sanitary pads. It is also reassuring to know the facts.

When you get your growth spurt during puberty, you might find you grow about 2–4 inches (6–11 cm) taller in a year if you are a girl, or 3–5 inches (7–12 cm) if you are a boy.

CHECK IT OUT

A growth spurt is when you grow quickly in a short period of time. You will probably notice this when you start middle school and suddenly many of the girls are taller than most of the boys (because girls generally start puberty earlier). Like the rest of the changes that occur during puberty, growth spurts happen at different times for different people, but things even out eventually.

When does puberty happen?

Most people worry that puberty is happening too early or too late, or that they will never grow or never stop growing. Everyone goes through puberty—they just do it at different times and at different rates. The age when people hit puberty varies between boys and girls, and also between individuals. Most girls begin puberty between the ages of 8 and 14, and most boys tend to start between 10 and 18 years old, but some people begin earlier and others later.

The rate at which puberty happens also differs. You might find one friend starts and finishes developing before many of your other friends have even started. Some people go through puberty in a year or less, while others may take up to six years. This is normal. It is not a race. Starting earlier is no better or worse than starting later. Everyone is different, so it stands to reason that we all experience puberty differently, too.

There is no "one size fits all" with puberty, and everyone experiences it slightly differently, but being fully informed will help you deal with it.

Alien bodies

When you hit puberty it can feel as if your body is being taken over by an alien species! Pimples, hairy spots, big feet and a weird new body shape—there are so many changes that when you look in a mirror you may not even recognize yourself. But don't worry—even though the changes that happen in puberty can be pretty dramatic, they are all perfectly normal.

Gorilla syndrome?

One day you'll look down in the shower and see hair where there was no hair before. Hair growth is one of the first obvious signs of puberty. Pubic hair usually appears first (the pubic area is around your genitals). Pubic hair is not as soft as the hair on your head, and although it is light and thin at first, it usually becomes darker and curlier. Underarm hair usually sprouts next. The hair on your arms and legs may also grow a bit longer, especially on boys. Boys grow hair on their chest and face, too.

Everyone becomes hairier during puberty, some more so than others…

CHECK IT OUT

During a growth spurt, the body grows so fast that the brain may not be able to keep up! When you grow taller, your center of gravity is higher. It takes a while for your brain to work out how to balance at this new height. This is why many teenagers feel clumsy.

Hair growth happens at different times and at different rates, and the amount, color or length of hair you have does not make you any more or less masculine or feminine than the next person.

Is that really me?

In puberty there is hardly one part of the body that does not change. The arms and legs get longer, and the hands and feet get bigger. Muscles grow bigger and stronger, especially on boys. People tend to put on weight during puberty, too, and the distribution of fat around the body changes. For boys, the shoulders become broader, and girls develop curves. Even the shape of the face changes—it goes from round to oval—and for boys, the nose and jaw become larger and more noticeable. Everyone changes height and shape at different rates. It's easy to feel like you will end up looking much taller or much shorter than average. Be patient and wait—most people continue to develop until the age of about 18.

MY BLOG

>
I got really stressed about the way I looked when I was 11. You just want to be the same as your friends, but I was taller than everyone, my feet were huge and I felt gross and totally left out. Then people started to catch up with me and now I'm just average height and feel OK about myself again.

JESS, 15

For some reason feet grow fastest of all! But there's no need to run away to join a circus—your feet also stop growing first so you "grow into them" eventually.

Why is this happening to me?

The reason for the changes is to turn you into an adult and prepare your body so that it is capable of reproducing (having children) when you are older. The triggers for all the changes that occur during puberty are hormones.

How hormones work

Hormones are chemical substances that create and control many of the changes that happen in your body. They are released by your glands and carried all over the body by your blood. When you're ready to begin puberty, the pituitary gland, a pea-shaped gland at the base of your brain, makes and releases growth hormones. These stimulate the growth of your bones and body. The pituitary gland also triggers other glands to release the hormones that make you develop what are called secondary sexual characteristics—the external and internal changes that turn you into an adult man or woman.

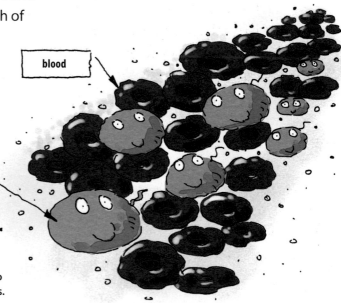

brain

pituitary gland

blood

hormones

Hormones are often compared to chemical messengers, traveling fast through the blood vessels inside your body to carry important information and instructions to other areas.

In boys, hormones from the pituitary stimulate the testes glands to produce testosterone. Testosterone is one of the hormones that makes boys' voices deepen and starts the growth of body hair. Testosterone and hormones from the pituitary gland together also trigger the production of sperm cells in the testes. In girls, two glands called the ovaries produce tiny eggs, called ova, and hormones, such as estrogen, cause the changes that come with puberty. To reproduce, a sperm from a male must join with and fertilize an egg from a female. (There is more about sexual reproduction on pages 32–33.)

Quiz

Try this quiz to test your knowledge of what puberty is.
(Answers on page 61)

1. Puberty starts

a) when the pituitary gland in the brain sends signals to your body telling it to produce sex hormones.

b) when you start middle school.

c) when you start to get taller.

2. How long does puberty take?

a) It varies, depending on the person.

b) One or two years.

c) It stops when you have a baby.

3. What is a growth spurt?

a) The short period of rapid growth that you experience during puberty.

b) It is a medical condition.

c) It is the race boys have to see who can get tallest first.

4. During puberty a boy can grow 3–5 inches (7–12 cm) taller in

a) one year.

b) one month.

c) one week.

5. The sex hormones responsible for puberty in females and males are

a) estrogen (girls) and testosterone (boys).

b) growth hormones.

c) ovaries (girls) and testes (boys).

Breasts, bras and hair

Girls will notice some big changes during puberty. Some of these affect the way they look on the outside—they are likely to develop larger breasts and a curvier body shape, for example. Some changes, such as starting periods, happen on the inside.

Taking shape

The first sign of puberty in most girls is that their breasts start to grow. This usually starts between the ages of 8 and 13. Breasts can continue to grow until women are in their early 20s. The reason women have breasts is to produce milk to feed a baby. Breasts grow bigger because, during puberty, fat builds up around glands called mammaries that may eventually make the milk.

TOP TIP

Buying bras

Bras are vital once girls begin to develop breasts. They protect and support breasts when you are doing everyday things, such as running for the bus. They also help to give you a nice shape and make you feel more comfortable when wearing close-fitting clothes. Although it may be embarrassing to start with, the best way to buy a bra is to be measured in a fitting room. Ask for advice about what sort of bra would suit your lifestyle and try on a few styles until you find some that feel and look right.

Buying a bra from a store that offers advice and guidance will ensure you don't make mistakes when choosing a new bra.

Girls may also notice that as they grow older, their nipples grow darker and larger. Their hips may become wider and their waist smaller. Many girls also develop a more rounded stomach, buttocks and legs, and these changes give their body a curvier, more womanly shape.

Hair where?

As well as the change in shape, another change is that many girls become hairier. The hair on their arms and legs gets darker, and they start to grow hair under their armpits and around the pubic area (around the genital region). Girls may also grow darker hair above their lips, around their nipples and a line of darker hair running between their belly button and pubic hair. (See page 20 for information about dealing with or disguising unwanted hair.)

Body issues

Many girls feel self-conscious about their bodies during puberty. They worry that their breasts are too small or too large, or that their bodies are too skinny or too curvy. The fact is that breasts, bottoms, and hips come in different shapes and sizes—there is no one ideal shape or size. The differences you see among your friends happen because of their genes and their natural body shape. It is normal to have nipples that point in or nipples that point out, for example, and for one breast to grow more quickly than the other. They usually even out eventually, at least enough so that no one else will notice.

It's perfectly normal for girls to develop curves at different ages and different rates.

> **MY BLOG**
>
> I grew up a lot faster than all of my friends. I needed a bra long before any of them, and I felt like everyone was talking about me or staring at my chest. After I got a bra I felt better, and then suddenly all the other girls started to develop and no one paid any attention to me any more.
>
> KATE, 15

11

The female body

When people buy a new gadget, they usually get an owner's guide to tell them how it works. Both girls and boys need to know and understand how their own body and that of the opposite sex work to understand the changes that happen.

On the outside

Your external sex organs are the ones you can see. In women, the entire outside genital area is called the vulva. The vulva includes the inner and outer vaginal labia, the clitoris and the openings of the urethra and of the vagina. Across the opening of the vagina there is a very thin sheet of skin tissue called the hymen. This has holes in it that gradually get bigger as girls grow older, until the hymen breaks down altogether. The labia are often called lips, and these folds of skin help to protect the other parts of the vulva. The outer labia are usually partly covered in pubic hair and the inner labia are thinner. The small, bud-like part at the top of the inner labia is called the clitoris.

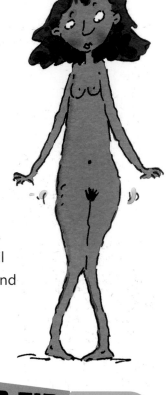

External female sex organs

clitoris

outer labia—two flaps of soft skin that fold over the rest of the vulva to protect it

urethral opening

inner labia

vaginal opening

anus

TOP TIP

When you have a quiet moment, behind locked doors in a bathroom or bedroom, take a hand mirror and take a look at your outer sex organs. Although you might feel a bit silly or embarrassed at first, this is a good way to learn the basics about your body.

The urethral opening and anus are not part of the sex organs. The anus is the hole where solid body wastes (feces) leave the body and the urethral opening is where liquid waste (urine) comes out.

This side view shows where the openings from a girl's outer sex organs go on the inside of her body.

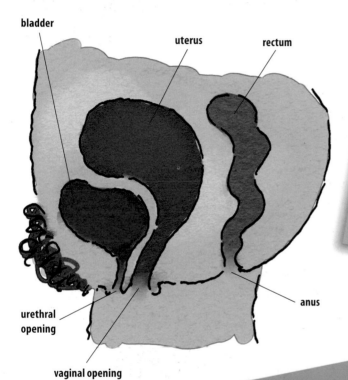

bladder

uterus

rectum

anus

urethral opening

vaginal opening

CHECK IT OUT, GIRLS

The clitoris is highly sensitive, and rubbing or touching it can feel good. Touching yourself for pleasure in this way is called masturbation. Masturbation is perfectly normal and does your body no harm. Many girls masturbate, but just as many do not.

CHECK IT OUT

Before girls start their periods they may notice a sticky, colorless or milky liquid coming out of their vagina. This is vaginal discharge, and it is nothing to worry about. It is perfectly normal—the walls of the vagina produce this liquid to keep the vaginal area moist and to protect it against damage or infection. The only time to worry is if the discharge smells very bad, becomes heavy or thick, or changes color. This may happen because you have an infection, so it is best to see your doctor.

What are periods?

During puberty the sex organs inside the body also grow bigger, and for girls, their periods, or menstrual cycles, start. Some girls are excited about getting their period because they feel more like a woman; others feel nervous about it. The important thing to remember is that it's a good thing—it means the girl is developing properly and becoming a woman.

When do they start?

Most girls start their periods between the ages of 9 and 16, but some start earlier than that. Many girls start their period at a similar age to when their mother started or about two years after their breasts start to develop, but it is a bit unpredictable.

What happens?

After a girl's periods start, roughly once a month, one of the ovaries releases an egg. The egg travels down its Fallopian tube to the womb, also known as the uterus. If an egg is fertilized by sperm (see pages 32–33), it may develop into a baby within the uterus. Just in case this happens, the uterus builds up its inner lining with extra blood and extra tissue to nourish and protect the baby as it develops. Most of the time, however, these tissues and cells are not needed by the body and they flow out of the vagina as a blood-like fluid. This blood flow, or period, can last for anywhere between two and seven days. Even though this is called menstrual bleeding and the blood loss can seem heavy, remember that the body is getting rid of extra blood and tissue, so menstrual bleeding is not the same as bleeding after an injury.

TOP TIP

When your periods begin, it can help to make a note in your diary of when they start and finish so you know roughly when to expect the next one. That way you can always make sure you are prepared and have sanitary pads or tampons at the ready (see pages 16–17). If you are worried your period is too heavy (this is rarely a problem—it is just that some girls bleed more heavily than others), you should see your doctor.

Settling down

Most periods happen once a month or every three to five weeks, but for the first year at least they are unlikely to be regular. A menstrual cycle—the time between the first day of one period and the first day of the next—could be as short as three weeks, or as long as six weeks or more. Even once the menstrual cycle has settled into a regular pattern, girls can miss a period if they are ill, exercising heavily, or stressed or upset about something, such as exams. However, a missed period can also mean that the girl is pregnant if she has been sexually active. If this happens, it is important for her to see a doctor right away.

This is how a girl or woman's internal sex organs look from the front.

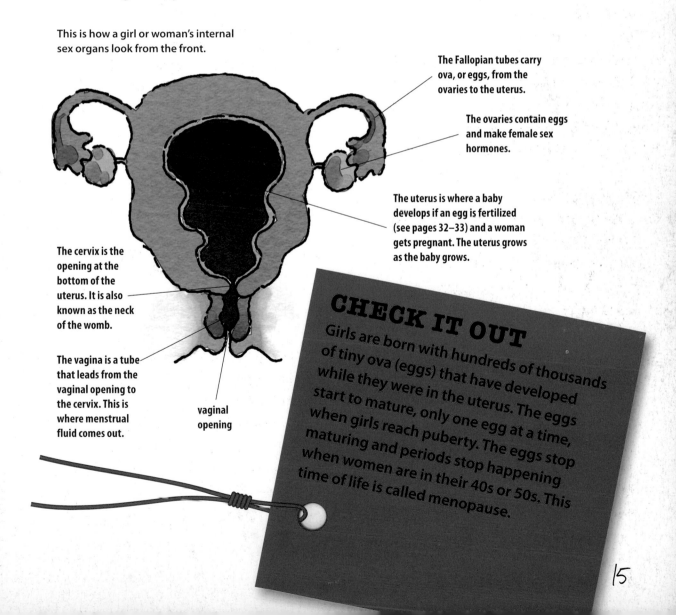

The Fallopian tubes carry ova, or eggs, from the ovaries to the uterus.

The ovaries contain eggs and make female sex hormones.

The uterus is where a baby develops if an egg is fertilized (see pages 32–33) and a woman gets pregnant. The uterus grows as the baby grows.

The cervix is the opening at the bottom of the uterus. It is also known as the neck of the womb.

The vagina is a tube that leads from the vaginal opening to the cervix. This is where menstrual fluid comes out.

vaginal opening

CHECK IT OUT

Girls are born with hundreds of thousands of tiny ova (eggs) that have developed while they were in the uterus. The eggs start to mature, only one egg at a time, when girls reach puberty. The eggs stop maturing and periods stop happening when women are in their 40s or 50s. This time of life is called menopause.

Coping with periods

Most girls use either tampons, sanitary pads or both to soak up the menstrual blood during a period, and to keep it from getting onto their clothes.

Sanitary pads and tampons

Sanitary pads fit inside girls' panties. Most pads have a sticky strip on the underside that attaches the pad to the panties and some pads come with "wings," which are sticky flaps that wrap around the underside of the panties for extra security. A tampon is a small, finger-shaped cotton pad with a string at one end. The tampon is pushed into the vagina with the string hanging outside the body. This string can be pulled to take out the tampon later on. Some tampons also have cardboard or plastic applicators that help to insert the tampon.

TOP TIP

Try out different brands and sizes of tampons and pads to find the ones that suit you. To avoid infection, change pads and tampons often—at least three or four times a day and more on heavy days—and avoid wearing a tampon at night.

Some girls and women prefer pads because they don't like inserting tampons. The advantage tampons have over pads is that they are invisible once they are inside and can be worn with tight-fitting clothes. They can also be used during swimming or other watersports. Many girls start off with pads and try tampons later, but as with so many other things to do with puberty, there are no right or wrong choices.

Having your period should not stop you from doing your normal activities, even if your favorite sport is swimming.

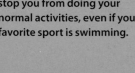

Heavy or light?

Many girls and women find that their blood flow is heavier at the beginning of their period and lighter toward the end. There are thicker or bigger pads and tampons for the heavy times and thinner ones for lighter days. Panty liners, which are very thin sanitary pads, can be used at the end of the period when there may be a day or two of very light bleeding, called spotting. At the start of their period, when they may have a very heavy flow, many girls and women use a tampon and a pad at the same time.

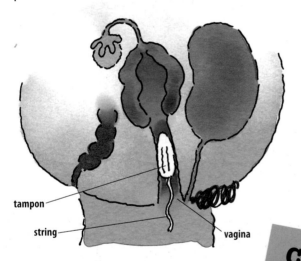

tampon

string

vagina

To insert a tampon for the first time, relax and breathe slowly. Insert the tampon gradually and gently into your vagina. Push it in a finger's length or until comfortable and make sure you leave the string on the outside of your vagina so that you can remove the tampon later. To make insertion easier the first few times, you could lubricate the rounded end of the tampon with a water-based jelly, such as K-Y Jelly, which you can buy from the drugstore.

TOP TIPS

● If your period catches you by surprise and you don't have a pad or tampon with you, you could use a wad of soft tissues or rolled-up toilet paper. Then ask a friend or the school nurse for a pad or buy one from a machine in a public restroom.

● If you leak on your clothes, take your sweater off and tie it around your waist until you can change your clothes.

● It is fine to bathe or shower without a sanitary pad. You will lose only the tiniest amount of blood in the water. Remove your pad before the bath or shower and put a new one on afterward.

CHECK IT OUT, GIRLS

When it is time to dispose of your sanitary items, do not flush pads down the toilet. Not only can they block the pipes but they are also bad for the environment. Most restrooms have a waste disposal box for sanitary pads and often little bags to put them in before you dispose of them. You can flush tampons down the toilet, but it is much better to wrap them in tissue or a bag and dispose of them in a waste basket.

Other period stuff

Many girls find they have some kind of discomfort before, during, or after their periods. They may get cramps, a bloated feeling in the stomach, sore or swollen breasts, abdominal or back pain or headaches. Everyone is different and not all girls will experience all or any of these things. However, there are ways to help make these symptoms more bearable.

To help with pain

Exercise, either sports or gentle stretching, can help with cramps and other pains during your period. Girls who get tender breasts could try wearing a more supportive bra during their period. For period pains, an old-fashioned hot water bottle on the tummy can help. You can also buy stick-on heat pads to wear under your jeans, which can target the pain. Sometimes, a painkiller will help, but you should always check with your parent or guardian before taking any medication.

TOP TIP

Lots of girls feel self-conscious around the time of their period because they are worried that they smell. This is rarely the case, but it is a good idea to wash your vaginal area every day, especially during your period, to prevent infections from developing. Always wash and dry from front to back to avoid spreading bacteria from the anus to the vagina (this is also why it's best to wipe front to back when you go to the barhroom).

You may find that you feel extra hungry and get food cravings around the time of your period, but try to stick to a healthy diet.

Premenstrual syndrome (PMS)

As well as the physical discomfort, periods can also affect moods, and girls can be more emotional just before they start their period. They may feel moody, irritable, tearful or tired, and they may find it hard to concentrate. Doctors are not 100 percent certain why premenstrual syndrome (PMS) happens, but one theory is that the changing levels of hormones that occur in the menstrual cycle have an effect on the chemicals in the brain that control the body's moods.

PMS can be eased by doing a few simple things. Avoiding stressful situations when a period is due can help. For example, instead of letting a backlog of homework build up, be prepared and get the homework out of the way the week before a period is due. Girls can also be extra kind to themselves by taking a bubble bath or going to bed early with a favorite book or magazine. They should also try not to be too hard on themselves if they lose their temper. It can help to explain the situation to other people—just saying sorry to someone for snapping at them and explaining that you have PMS can help.

Some girls find that they are a little moodier and more short-tempered around the time of their period…

CHECK IT OUT

Toxic shock syndrome is a very rare type of blood poisoning caused by bacteria, and it happens to a very small number of women who use tampons. The symptoms include a headache and sore throat, aching muscles and high temperature, vomiting, diarrhea, confusion and dizziness, or a rash.

19

Girl talk

When girls get darker underarm and leg hair, hair around their bikini line and possibly on the upper lip, they may choose to be natural and leave it or they may want to remove the hair.

MY BLOG

>

I started to grow hair under my arms when I was only nine. I had to start shaving because my friends noticed and I got really embarrassed. I only shave now when I really need to, like when I go to the beach. Everyone should feel comfortable with themselves the way they are, so I would say shaving is your choice but I'd only do it when you have to.

SUZIE, 13

There are many ways to remove unwanted hair. They vary in price, time taken and pain!

SHAVING: This is quick, cheap, and painless if done carefully (with a clean razor on soapy, wet skin). However, the stubble that grows back can be itchy and cause skin irritation. Girls should never shave facial hair.

HAIR REMOVAL CREAM: This is painless because it dissolves hair at the roots. The regrowth is softer than after shaving, but the cream is more expensive than shaving and can irritate the skin.

PLUCKING: This is cheap and regrowth is slow, but it would take weeks to pluck legs! Hair around the nipples needs to be trimmed with a small, clean pair of scissors—plucking these hairs can cause ingrown hairs and infection.

WAXING: This can be done at home or in a salon. The regrowth is slow and after time, the hairs will become finer. However, some people find it painful and it is expensive.

ELECTROLYSIS: This has to be done in a salon and is very pricey, but it is permanent.

BLEACHING: Bleaching dark hairs to blend in with the surrounding skin is an alternative to hair removal. It is painless but will not work very well if you have darker skin.

To avoid razor nicks, take your time when shaving.

Yeast and bladder infections

Yeast and bladder infections are two common conditions that girls should be aware of. A yeast infection makes the vagina itchy and sore. It causes a thick, white, smelly discharge and it makes it painful to urinate. Seeing a doctor is important to confirm that you actually have a yeast infection before you buy over-the-counter treatments.

A bladder infection causes the bladder to be inflamed. It makes you want to urinate often but only a few drops of urine come out. A burning sensation when urinating, cloudy urine, a slight fever and back or tummy pain are all symptoms. Drinking lots of water can help, but it's best to see a doctor.

Quiz

How many can you get right?
(Answers on page 61)

1. **The first sign of puberty in most girls is that their breasts start to grow.**
   True or false?

2. **Your periods start when your ovaries start to produce eggs.**
   True or false?

3. **When your periods first begin they are often irregular.**
   True or false?

4. **You should change a tampon at least once every four to eight hours.**
   True or false?

5. **It is fine to flush used sanitary pads down the toilet.**
   True or false?

6. **PMS stands for Perfect Menstrual Situation.**
   True or false?

7. **Exercise can help get rid of period pains.**
   True or false?

8. **The best way for girls to get rid of facial hair is to shave.**
   True or false?

Hair and Adam's apple

There are some puberty changes—both inside and outside—that happen only to boys to turn them into men. For example, they become more hairy and their voice deepens. The other major changes happen inside or below the waist, and some of them may make boys feel as if their private parts are not so private anymore!

Hair today, gone tomorrow

One of the first signs of puberty in boys is hair growth. During puberty boys are likely to grow hair on their face and underarms and thick coarse hair in the pubic area (above the penis). The hair on their arms and legs will get thicker and darker. Near the end of puberty or afterward, some boys grow chest hair, too, but not all men have chest hair. Many boys and men shave the hair on their face but others leave it to grow a mustache or beard. To avoid infections, boys should use shaving cream and a clean razor to shave, and avoid sharing razors or shavers.

Many boys and men shave off their facial hair, but most leave the rest of their body hair as it is.

MY BLOG

>

When I was 13 my nipples felt sore and started to grow and I was scared I was growing breasts like a girl or something! I feel a bit crazy for worrying about it now because eventually they settled down and someone told me it was normal and it was just my chest changing and getting bigger. Wish I'd known that at the time!

MATT, 15

Voice changes

Boys' voices are affected during puberty, too. Midway through a conversation, they may suddenly sound like a strangled cat, or a set of bagpipes. This means that the voice is "cracking," or changing into an adult's deeper tones. Your voice comes from throat muscles called vocal chords, located inside the voicebox, or larynx. As boys grow into men, these vocal chords get thicker and so the pitch of the voice gets lower or deeper. Boys have those strange squeaky moments when they are speaking because the larynx and vocal chords are adapting to the changes. The squeaking stops when their voice has settled into its deeper, lower tone.

CHECK IT OUT, BOYS

The other change you will notice in your throat is the Adam's apple, the lump in the front of your neck, which is part of your voicebox or larynx. As your vocal chords get bigger, the larynx becomes bigger, too, and often it is so big that it bulges out of your neck slightly. You could have a big Adam's apple, a small one or you may not have one at all—everyone is different.

The Adam's apple got its name from the story of the Garden of Eden, in which Adam ate a piece of the forbidden fruit and it got stuck in his throat.

23

Inside a boy's body

There are changes happening inside boys' bodies before they notice the changes that happen on the outside. The organs on the inside are the reproductive organs and the ones on the outside are the genitals.

Male sex organs

The first thing that boys may notice is that their testicles (or "balls") get bigger. The testicles are egg-shaped glands contained inside the wrinkly sacks of skin known as the scrotum. During puberty, the testicles grow to the size and shape of smallish plums. The testicles hang on the outside of the body in order to keep the sperm they contain just below normal body temperature. Boys may find that they have one testicle that hangs a little lower than the other. This is normal and a clever design that means they are less likely to knock into each other!

Within about a year, the penis starts to grow thicker and longer. The penis contains a tube called the urethra, through which urine passes from the bladder. Sperm also passes out of the penis when boys or men ejaculate. (For more information about this see pages 26–27.)

TOP TIP

Your testicles are easily hurt because they hang outside the body. You probably already know this if you have ever been kicked there by mistake during a game of soccer or other sports. Protect yourself by wearing a sports cup when you play contact sports such as football or when you bat during a baseball game.

CHECK IT OUT

Some boys have part of or the entire foreskin removed in an operation that is usually performed when they are babies. This is called circumcision and it is sometimes done for religious reasons; for example, many Jewish and Muslim boys are circumcised. Circumcision has no effect on the normal functioning of the penis.

The glans is the area at the tip of the penis that contains the opening through which urine comes out. The foreskin is a fold of skin that covers the glans, and it feels sensitive and tender.

Making sperm

The internal sex organs are mostly involved with the production or movement of sperm, the male reproductive cells. The testicles are the sperm-making units, and during puberty they start to produce millions of sperm each day. The other internal sex organs store the sperm (the epididymis), carry the sperm from the testicles to the urethra (vas deferens), or produce fluids that keep the sperm healthy (seminal vesicles and prostate gland). Once the testicles have started producing sperm, they usually go on producing it for the man's whole life.

The genitals or sexual organs of a circumcised male.

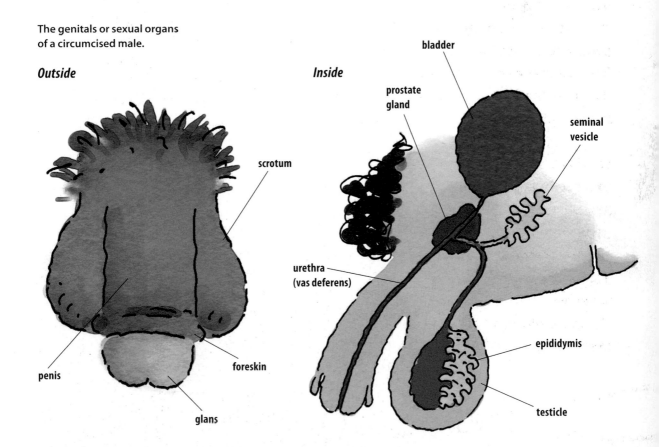

Outside

Inside

scrotum

penis

foreskin

glans

bladder

prostate gland

seminal vesicle

urethra (vas deferens)

epididymis

testicle

A mind of its own?

During puberty, boys can feel as if their penis has a mind of its own. They may find that they get an erection—when the penis becomes stiff and hard—when they least expect it. This is all because of the hormones in the boy's body.

All about erections

When the body starts producing more sex hormones, boys have more sexual feelings. These feelings lead to erections, which enable men to reproduce in the future. The trouble is that during puberty boys can also get an erection at other times, and sometimes at awkward moments—like when they are on a bus or sitting in class. Erections can happen just because a boy is feeling happy or warm, or simply because there is a rush of sex hormones running through his body. Boys may feel embarrassed when this happens, but it is perfectly normal. Relaxing and crossing the legs will help erections go away after a couple of minutes.

Erections happen when blood vessels in the penis widen to let more blood flow into the spongy tissue inside the penis. Then muscles around the penis constrict (tighten) to keep the penis hard. It's kind of like the way a balloon enlarges and gets firmer when you fill it with water.

CHECK IT OUT

- Every day an average adult man makes between 50 and 500 million sperm cells.
- Individual sperm are so tiny that they can be seen only under a microscope.
- During ejaculation, a man produces about a teaspoonful of semen. This might contain up to 400 million sperm cells.

How ejaculation works

During an erection, boys may also experience ejaculation. Ejaculation is when sperm cells pass quickly from the epididymis along the vas deferens up toward the penis. Along the way, fluids from the seminal vesicles and the prostate gland mix with the sperm to form a milky liquid called semen. The semen passes into the urethra and is ejaculated (or spurts) out of the tip of the penis. Sperm cells that are not ejaculated stay in the testicles for about three weeks before being absorbed back into the body.

TOP TIP

If you have an erection you may have to wait before passing urine. When your penis is hard, a muscle closes off the urethra from the bladder so that you can never pass urine at the same time as you ejaculate. This means urine can never mix with sperm in the urethra.

If you're standing up when you get an unwanted erection, reach for something like a bag or a book and casually hold it in front of your groin until the problem goes away.

27

Boy talk

One of the things almost all boys worry about at one time or another is whether their penis is "normal." Is it too small or too big? Is it a strange shape?

Size and shape

Sometimes, boys compare their penis size with that of their friends. This is a mistake. To begin with, the penis will be a different size in different situations. When it is cold, the penis shrinks a bit, and when it is erect, it grows in size. It is also perfectly normal to have a penis that bends or curves a bit to one side.

The reality is that the size or shape of the penis has nothing to do with manliness. So long as it works properly, it will not affect a man's ability to have sex. Research shows that by the time boys are adults, most penises are roughly the same size (about 5 inches [11–13 cm] long) when they are fully erect.

Even if you think your penis is on the small side, you'll be surprised how different it looks when it is erect!

MY BLOG

>
I thought my penis was smaller than everyone else's beginning when I was in grade school. It used to really screw me up and I wouldn't shower after sports in case people noticed. Now I know that some guys have penises that are as long limp as they are when erect, but others (like mine) shrink right down when they're not erect. I just wish I hadn't wasted so much time worrying about it.

RICO, 16

What are wet dreams?

Wet dreams are when boys ejaculate while they are sleeping. The first thing they may know about this is when they wake up to find that their sheets or pajama pants are wet. This is perfectly natural and normal. At least eight out of ten males have wet dreams. Boys probably have several erections a night without knowing it, and most teenagers have a wet dream once a month or more. Wet dreams are just a fact of life and they stop as boys grow older.

Dreams do not necessarily have anything to do with your real desires...

What is masturbation?

Masturbation is when a boy gives himself an erection and makes himself ejaculate (or "come") by stroking or rubbing his penis. Most men and boys find out that touching the penis gives them a pleasant, tingling sensation. When they masturbate, these feelings get stronger and stronger until the boy or man ejaculates. The wave or rush of excitement that they feel when they ejaculate is also known as an orgasm or climax. There is nothing wrong or harmful about masturbating, however much it is done. It's also perfectly normal not to masturbate—some people do, others do not. However, masturbation is very personal and should be done in private.

TOP TIP

Don't panic if you realize you have wet dreams when you dream about your school principal or other unlikely people or scenarios. Just because you have a dream about dancing naked around the gym with your PE teacher, it doesn't mean you really want to do it!

29

Need to know

There are a few more things that boys need to know about looking after their private parts...

Keep it clean

The foreskin, if the boy has one, is a space where grease and dirt can build up, so boys should wash under the foreskin every day. To do this, boys need to pull back the foreskin gently, wash the area beneath with warm water and non-perfumed soap and pat dry with a clean towel. This will also get rid of any smegma, the white, creamy stuff that is found under the foreskin. Smegma has a job to do—it keeps the glands and foreskin oiled and working smoothly—but it can give off a cheesy smell if the penis is not cleaned regularly.

One of the most important parts of personal hygiene for a boy is to keep his penis clean.

Lumps and bumps

Another thing that concerns boys and men is lumps and bumps on the penis. This is common and normal, and almost all are quite harmless. Some bumps (usually lower down the penis) are sebaceous glands at the base of hair follicles, glands

Here are some common complaints boys should know about:

BLUE BALLS: The balls may look bluish because blood fills the blood vessels in the testicles. This leads to an uncomfortable feeling in the testicles that you can get with an erection if you don't ejaculate. It does not last long.

INFLAMED FORESKIN: If you get sore, red, itchy glans, you may have a bacterial infection. Keep yourself extra clean and if it doesn't go away after a couple of days, see a doctor.

JOCK ITCH: If you get a red, itchy rash around your groin, you may have jock itch, a condition caused by the same fungus that causes athlete's foot. Get a spray or cream from the doctor to treat it.

THRUSH: If you have a red, sore, itchy penis with a smelly discharge, you may have a fungal infection called thrush. Doctors can supply a cream to clear it up.

that secrete oil into the hairs. Small, hard white bumps on the head of the penis are also normal and harmless—although picking at them could cause an infection—so leave them alone.

Once in a while a boy may get a pimple on his penis, which will go away just like any other pimples. However, when a boy is sexually active, spots on the penis can be a sign that he has a sexually transmitted infection (STI), such as herpes or genital warts, and he needs to see a doctor immediately. (For more about STIs see pages 40–41.)

Quiz

So how much do you really know about the male body? (Answers on page 61.)

1. One of the first signs of puberty in boys is hair growth. Where does this extra hair grow?
a) The face, underarms and around the base of the penis.
b) All over the body.
c) Under the nose and on the chin.

2. What causes an erection?
a) A bone inside the penis.
b) Increased blood flow into the penis.
c) Flow of sperm into the penis.

3. Sperm cells are produced by
a) the urethra.
b) the testicles.
c) the prostate gland.

4. What is the difference between sperm and semen?
a) There is no difference; they are just different names for the same thing.
b) Sperm are the reproductive cells; semen is the creamy fluid in which sperm swim.
c) Sperm comes from the testicles and semen is the white stuff found under the foreskin.

5. Men stop producing sperm
a) at around 40 or 50, at the same age as women go through menopause.
b) never—they go on making sperm their entire lives.
c) when they are in their 70s.

What is sex?

The changes that happen to you in puberty turn you into an adult capable of reproducing, but what is sex all about? This chapter looks at how sex can make a woman pregnant, what the law says about having sex, and how contraception works. It also gives you answers to some of the questions you may have always wanted to ask…

How sexual intercourse works

When a man and woman have sex, they usually start out by kissing and touching each other. This is called foreplay. Taking time for foreplay is important because it arouses and prepares the couple's bodies for intercourse. In men it causes an erection. In women it stimulates glands in the vagina to produce extra moisture. When they are ready, the man puts his erect penis into the woman's vagina, which stretches so that the penis can fit inside it comfortably. Then the couple move in such a way that the man's penis slides back and forth inside the woman's vagina. This gives feelings of pleasure that grow stronger and stronger. Both the man and the woman may have an orgasm, often at different times, when these feelings reach a peak and then stop. For men, this involves ejaculation. After a man has ejaculated, his penis goes back to its normal size and he can slide it out of the woman's vagina.

CHECK IT OUT

Some people think that they won't get pregnant on their first time, if they have sex standing up, if they have sex during the woman's period, or if the man pulls out before ejaculating. Don't be fooled: it takes just one sperm, and it can happen in any encounter in which semen gets inside a woman's body.

It's worth going over the facts about sex and conception again because you may not have been paying attention in biology class.

Conception

Once inside a woman, sperm swim through the cervix and the uterus, toward the Fallopian tubes. Most sperm don't make it that far, or they may go up the Fallopian tube that does not contain an egg, or ovum, (only one egg is released into one of the tubes each month), but those that do, race to locate the egg. Very often, no sperm make it, but if one sperm does reach the egg and manages to push its way inside, the genetic material of the sperm and egg fuse together. This is the moment of conception, or the formation of a new life. The egg then creates a chemical barrier to keep other sperm out. The egg is now fertilized and moves slowly down the Fallopian tube into the uterus, where it starts to develop into an embryo, the early stage of a baby.

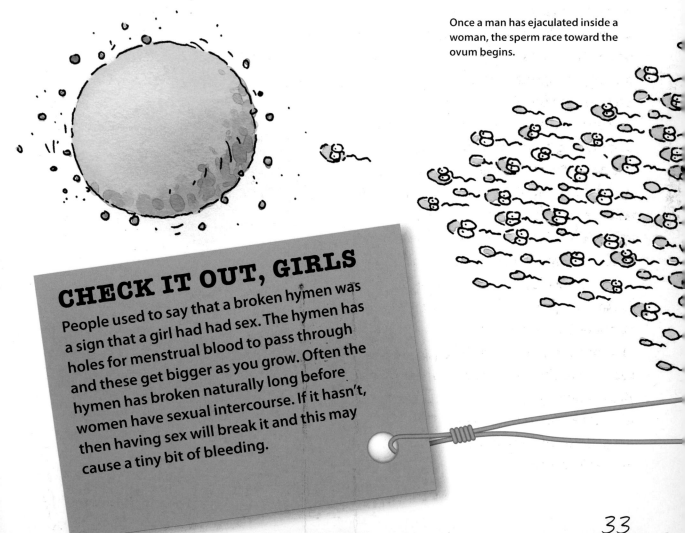

Once a man has ejaculated inside a woman, the sperm race toward the ovum begins.

CHECK IT OUT, GIRLS

People used to say that a broken hymen was a sign that a girl had had sex. The hymen has holes for menstrual blood to pass through and these get bigger as you grow. Often the hymen has broken naturally long before women have sexual intercourse. If it hasn't, then having sex will break it and this may cause a tiny bit of bleeding.

Sex and you

You may be mature and know your own mind. Maybe you think that as long as you use contraception, it is nobody else's business to tell you when you are ready to have sex. However, you need to know how the law affects you and what to consider when making your choices.

What the law says

One of the most important things to know about sex is that in the United States there are laws regarding the age of consent. This is the age at which people are legally allowed to have sex—between ages 16 and 18, depending on the state. The law is in place to protect and guide you. If you are under the age of consent, you may be physically ready to have sex but it's unlikely that you are emotionally ready, even if you feel that you are. On the other hand, even if you have reached the age of consent, you will not necessarily be ready either. Many people choose to wait until they are well into their teens or twenties—or even until they're married—before they have sex.

The law is there to help you. Before you decide to have sex, find out about the age of consent in your state and talk to your partner and doctor about the different kinds of contraception.

MY BLOG

>

After I decided I was not going to have sex until I was older, I felt good about my decision. I found I could relax and talk to guys more easily and most guys (and girls) respected my choice and me more because of it.

ZOE, 16

Ready or not?

If you have sex too young, it may make you feel bad about yourself and leave you with bad memories or an unwanted pregnancy. Most people prefer to wait until they are older and until they find someone they really care about and have built up a relationship with over a period of time. Do not become someone who has sex for the wrong reasons. Some people do it because they think everyone else is doing it. In fact more than three-quarters of teenagers wait until they are older than 16 years of age. Some people do it to feel more grown-up or to brag about it. There are risks with this, such as the danger of catching a sexually transmitted infection or STI (for more information on STIs see pages 40–41) and the risk of getting a bad reputation, which could put off someone you really like.

TOP TIP

It can be hard to say no if someone you care about is trying to persuade you to have sex. It is your body and you should only have sex when you feel sure that it's the right time to do it and the right thing to do. If you are too young or not ready, then you should say no. You don't owe anybody an explanation as to why you are not ready. If someone says they care about you enough to want to have sex with you, they should also respect you enough to wait until you are ready. If they don't, then you have to question whether they are the right person to be with in the first place.

There's no need to resort to violence to stop a boyfriend who is being persistent about sex—just tell him how you feel!

Contraception

Getting pregnant is a life-changing event, especially when you are young. Having a baby usually disrupts education and career plans and keeps you at home when you could be out having a good time with your friends. The simplest and best way to avoid pregnancy is not to have sex, but it is useful to know about other methods of contraception.

About condoms

There are two different kinds of condoms, both of which are made from thin latex (rubber) or plastic. As well as helping to prevent unwanted pregnancies, latex condoms can also prevent sexually transmitted infections (STIs).

TOP TIP

If a couple finds it hard to talk about contraception or the man refuses to wear a condom, this is a sign that the couple isn't ready to have a sexual relationship. No one should even consider having sex before discussing and choosing a reliable method of contraception. Even so, no contraceptive is 100 percent reliable, so every time a couple has sex, there is still a small chance that the woman could get pregnant.

To avoid having children before you have the time, money, and energy that they take, make sure you are clued in about contraception.

The most common condom is the male condom. This fits like a sock over the penis and has to be unrolled onto a penis that is erect. Once the penis starts to go limp (after ejaculation, for example) the condom slides off and there is a risk that sperm will spill out, so you have to hold on to the condom and slide the penis out of the vagina before it goes limp.

The female condom fits inside the vagina. It is much less common and more difficult to use. Both types of condoms work by stopping sperm from reaching the egg, both MUST be put on before the penis gets anywhere near the vagina and both can be used only once. Condoms can be bought from drugstores and supermarkets.

To put a condom on correctly, roll it down to the base of the penis.

Other forms of contraception

Diaphragms and cervical caps are latex or silicone shapes that a woman inserts in her vagina to fit over her cervix as a barrier to sperm. Used with spermicidal creams, they stop sperm from reaching or fertilizing an egg. Contraceptive pills stop the ovaries from releasing an egg each month and make the uterus lining thinner and less able to accept an egg. There are also options such as injections, implants and devices that fit inside a woman's uterus. To find out more about them, talk to your doctor or someone at a family planning center. Many centers offer free and confidential advice.

CHECK IT OUT

Emergency contraceptive pills (ECPs) are tablets women can take to prevent pregnancy. They can be taken up to three days after having sex when a woman's regular contraception has failed—for example, if the condom has slipped off or broken. ECPs should be used only in an emergency or if no contraception was used. Check with your doctor or healthcare facility.

Keep safe

Sexual feelings can cause some people to use their strength, age or position in a family to force another person to do something sexual with them. It is your body, and whenever anyone forces you to do something against your will, it is wrong. You need to be aware of how to keep safe from dangers like these.

What is sexual abuse?

Sexual abuse is when someone forces or persuades another person to have sex or sexual contact with them against their will. This includes someone touching you in places that make you feel uncomfortable or that hurt, or telling you to take off your clothes. It also includes someone showing you sex films or pictures when you are alone with them, or talking to you in a sexual way.

Dealing with abuse

Victims of sexual abuse sometimes think they are to blame. They think that they must have led their abuser on in some way. Sexual abuse is never the victim's fault, no matter how friendly he or she was to the abuser before it happened and whoever the abuser is.

TOP TIPS

Most of the time you will be safe when you go out, but it's worth taking some precautions, especially at night:

● Never hitchhike. Instead, get a ride home from someone you know or stay at a friend's house, catch a bus or train, or take a cab, preferably with a friend. Make sure it is from a licensed cab company.
● Tell people where you are going, when you are going to be home and the route you intend to take.
● If you get stuck, call your parents, however late it is. They might be annoyed at first, but it's better to be safe than sorry.
● Walk along main, well-lit roads and avoid alleys or wooded or deserted areas. Stay alert—don't listen to music or talk on your cell phone, as you won't be able to hear if anyone is approaching.

38

If you or someone you know has been or is being abused, you must report it to a trustworthy adult, such as a parent or other adult relative, guardian, teacher, doctor or the police. This may be harder to do if the abuser is someone you know, especially if he or she is a family member. However, you have to go through with it to help that person and reduce the risk to other people who may be in danger. You can also get confidential advice from a variety of different organizations (see page 63) that have helpline counselors you can talk to for free.

Chatroom dangers

Many cases of sexual abuse have been traced back to Internet chatrooms. Talking to people online is risky because it is easy for them to lie. For example, there have been cases of older men pretending to be teenage boys to chat with a young girl or boy in order to meet and abuse them. To be safe, never put photographs or any personal details on a public site or give your personal details to anyone you don't already know in real life. Most importantly, never arrange to meet anyone that you know only through the Internet as this can be very dangerous.

If someone says something that you find offensive, shocking or inappropriate online, report it to your Internet service provider (ISP).

39

STIs

Infections that are usually passed from one person to another through sexual contact—or even, in the case of herpes, by kissing—are known as sexually transmitted infections (STIs) or sexually transmitted diseases (STDs). The problem with STIs is you often cannot tell if someone has one, or even if you have one.

Everyone feels a little embarrassed or shy when they have to talk about a personal problem, but doctors and nurses are used to dealing with these problems. They will not judge you and will respect your privacy.

CHECK IT OUT

Pubic lice and scabies are not STIs. They are tiny insects that can pass from person to person during sexual contact. They live on your skin and make you very itchy. You should be able to get rid of them by using a cream prescribed by a doctor.

Facts about some STIs:

CHLAMYDIA: This is a bacterial infection that causes rather vague symptoms, such as a whitish discharge and pain when urinating in both men and women. Women may get pain in the abdomen, heavier periods or bleeding between periods. It can be cured by antibiotics, but if left untreated, it can affect a woman's ability to have children.

GENITAL HERPES: This virus causes blisters and sores around the mouth, nose or eyes, or around the genitals and anus. Herpes can be spread through kissing or sexual contact. It can be treated with creams and tablets but often flares up again because once you have the virus, it remains in the body.

GONORRHEA: Also called "the clap," this bacterial infection causes discharge from the penis or vagina, pain when urinating and sometimes flu-like symptoms. If left untreated, it can affect a woman's ability to have children and may damage a man's testicles.

HIV/AIDS: HIV is a virus that destroys cells in the immune system. When the immune system is badly weakened, the patient is said to have AIDS. Because the body can no longer fight off serious infections, such as pneumonia, this can lead to death.

Signs and symptoms

If you have pain in your stomach or groin, rashes or itching in the groin area, problems or pain when you pass urine or any unusual discharges, get help. Talk to a parent and arrange to see a doctor or nurse. Don't try to self-diagnose yourself or ignore troublesome conditions. Be smart; get help.

TOP TIP

If you find that you do have an STI, do not have sexual contact with anyone until you have been treated and are no longer infectious. If you think that you may have passed the infection on to someone else, however embarrassing it is, tell them immediately so that they can be tested, too.

Quiz

How clued-in are you about sex?
(Answers on page 61)

1. **You can't get pregnant the first time you have sex.**
   True or false?

2. **Three-quarters of young people don't have sex until they are 16 or older.**
   True or false?

3. **A woman can't get pregnant if she or the man wears a condom during sex.**
   True or false?

4. **ECP stands for Extra Contraceptive Power.**
   True or false?

5. **The only way to be certain of not getting pregnant or catching an STI is not to have sex or sexual contact.**
   True or false?

6. **It's safe to meet up with someone you met in a chatroom if they have told you a lot about themselves.**
   True or false?

Dealing with emotions

Going through puberty is a bit like being on an emotional roller coaster. One minute you're flying high as a bird, the next you're down in the dumps. There are two reasons for these dramatic mood swings. One is the changing levels of hormones and the other is what is going on around you—for example, schoolwork and exams, competitions, issues with friends or parents.

Angry and frustrated?

Almost every teenager goes through rough patches, but what if your moods sometimes get the better of you? Some people's anger or frustration gets out of control and they take out their feelings on other people, perhaps by shouting or by using physical aggression. Or they may turn their anger or frustration in on themselves, causing them to shut off from other people, becoming depressed or in some cases hurt themselves.

CHECK IT OUT

It is normal to have times when you feel angry, frustrated and unhappy—everyone does. Depression, however, is when someone is very low for so long that it begins to affect every aspect of his or her life and he or she can no longer see a way out of it. Anyone who feels seriously depressed should talk to a parent, teacher, trusted adult friend or doctor.

If you feel the pressure is becoming too much for you, talk to someone about it. Don't let things go on as they are. Try to find other outlets for your feelings. Many people find that playing sports is a big help, especially martial arts or combat sports where they can channel their energy and aggression in a positive way. You might find that it helps to write down your feelings, perhaps in a letter to someone who has upset you. Even if you never send the letter, chances are that simply writing it will make you feel better.

Stress busters

One way to deal with stress is to find out what causes it and deal with or avoid those situations, or triggers, before they come along. For example, if schoolwork is becoming stressful, make a timetable for your homework. That way, you won't fall behind and can study so that you are fully prepared for any tests. If you are struggling with a subject, ask for extra help rather than struggling on alone. Don't be too hard on yourself if you fail a test or make a mistake—so long as you have tried your best, that is all you can do.

Like a roller-coaster ride, you may feel "up" one minute, and "down" the next, old enough to cope with anything one day and lost and helpless the day after. It is a difficult time, but it might make you feel better to know that everyone goes through it.

43

Problems with parents

Puberty is the time when you start to become more independent from your parents. You start to form your own ideas and develop your own identity with your own opinions and tastes. You may want to decide things for yourself, while your parents still think they need to be making decisions for you. This is a time of change and adjustment for both you and your parents that often leads to problems and friction. However, there are things you can do to improve matters.

Coming to a compromise

Parents lay down rules because they love you and don't want you to get hurt. Sometimes it seems like they worry too much, perhaps because of scare stories they read about or see on television, and then they may set rules that you think are unreasonable. Try talking to them calmly to see if you can come to a compromise. If you're going out, tell them where you're going and who you're going with. If you show that you are responsible, they may then be willing to compromise and let you stay out later or go out more often.

MY BLOG

>
My parents got really strict during my junior year. They wouldn't let me go out because they said I had to stay home and study. I stopped talking to them and that just made things worse. In the end my aunt persuaded them to give me more freedom. Though they were way too strict at first, I guess they were only trying to do what they thought was best for me.

JESS, 17

Sending your parents a text message or giving them a call to let them know you are safe will show them that you are responsible.

Communication

Sometimes you may feel like shouting and screaming at your parents because they just don't understand what is going on in your world. They might understand better if you tell them what is bothering you. Pick a quiet time and place, and be clear about any issues you have. For example, if something they do upsets you, explain why it does. If you're feeling stressed and that is making you crabby, telling them will help them be more understanding. Try to talk more to them about the little everyday things, too, or ask them how they are doing. Keeping the lines of communication open all the time will make it easier when you have something trickier to talk about.

Talking to your parents about everyday stuff—and even taking the time to ask what is going on in their lives—makes it easier to talk to them about bigger problems, too.

TOP TIP

Honesty really is the best policy! You don't have to tell your parents everything about your life, but it's not a good idea to lie to them. One lie—for example, saying you're at a friend's house when you're really going out to a club—can cost you their trust and that can lead to a clampdown on the amount of freedom you have.

45

Friendships

Friendships are important to everyone, but they are especially important when you're growing up. You can laugh with your friends and talk to them about all sorts of things because they are going through similar changes, and can understand where you're coming from. Friendships can also cause a few tricky problems.

It's great to have friends to talk things over with—most of the time…

Striking a balance

Friends are great, but you need to strike a balance in life. You still need to find time and energy for all the other things, such as schoolwork, exercise, chores and family. If you become too obsessed with your friends and all that is going on with them, you might neglect things such as studying, which is really important for your future.

Striking a balance also helps you to keep problems with friends in perspective. Some people can be a bit possessive and feel left out if a friend sees other people. Even best friends cannot be together all the time—they would probably become bored of each other if they did! If you develop other interests, you will be more independent and more relaxed about your friends having other interests, too.

TOP TIP

Sometimes you lose touch with old friends, or you may find that you don't share the same interests any more and you want to make new friends. If you find it hard to get to know new people, it can help to think of some things to talk about before you meet up with them. Ask them something about school or an activity in which they are involved. Find out if you have an interest or activity in common and steer the conversation toward that.

Feeling the pressure

Some friends may do things you feel uncomfortable with, such as smoking or drinking alcohol. They may put pressure on you to do those things, too. When someone tries to persuade you to do something you know or feel is wrong or that makes you feel bad about yourself, it is time to spend less time with these friends and make some new ones. This can be tough, but you need to trust your feelings. If something feels wrong, then it probably is wrong, and it's time to make a change.

Real friends don't push you into doing things such as smoking; they let you make your own decisions.

CHECK IT OUT

What makes a good friend?
● Good friends are loyal and don't talk about you behind your back.
● Good friends sometimes argue, but they also know how to apologize and forgive each other.
● Good friends make you feel great about yourself.
● Good friends value each other's opinions and don't try to make you do things you feel uncomfortable about.

More than friends?

Among your group of friends, have you suddenly found yourself especially attracted to one person in particular? Does just being near them make your heart race, your mouth dry and leave you weak at the knees? Don't worry—you have a crush and this is quite normal. During puberty, the sex hormones whizzing around your body make you interested in other people in a way you have never felt before.

Crushes and fantasies

You can have a crush on anyone—a friend, a celebrity or even a teacher. Crushes are your body's way of discovering what it feels like to be in love. It is also normal to think about your crush in a sexual way.

Having a crush can make it hard to concentrate on other things, but try not to let it take over your life.

48

Fantasies help you explore your new sexual feelings, but they don't necessarily mean you want to do those things for real. Having a crush can be exciting and fun, but if you get obsessed and think about them all the time it can start to get in the way. Don't neglect your friends, schoolwork and the other things you usually do.

Gay or straight?

Homosexuality, or being gay, is when a person has sexual feelings for someone of the same sex. Even if you find you have strong feelings for friends who are the same sex as you, this does not mean that you are gay. It is just part of your need to explore the different kinds of people you like and the different personalities to which you are attracted. During puberty your hormones and emotions are running high, so it's no wonder things can be intense with your friendships.

Some teenagers feel sure they are attracted from an early stage to people who are the same sex. Others may feel attracted to both sexes for a while. This is natural and caused by the hormones surging through your body. There is no need to label yourself too early. Give your hormones time to settle down and your true feelings will become clear to you. The most important thing is that you are comfortable with your sexual identity and that you respect other peoples' choices, too.

People often feel confused about the difference between having strong feelings for someone and wanting them to be their girlfriend or boyfriend.

MY BLOG

> I had a crush on a boy for like a term, but never had the guts to tell him. When I found out he was dating another girl, I was devastated. But I started meeting new people, and I found myself having crushes on other people and some of them liked me back! Now I think I only liked him because of his looks and that crushes are just a part of life…

JASMINE, 14

Going on dates

When you really like someone, and you think they like you, too, it may be time to work up the courage to ask them on a date. This can be exciting, but it can also be tough.

First step

To ask someone out on a date, try to pick a moment when he or she is alone. You could try starting up a casual conversation at first and then steer it toward an interest you share, such as action movies. Then you can ask them if they would like to go out sometime, maybe to the movies or to do something you both enjoy, such as bowling. If you have only just met, you could suggest doing something with a group of friends. That takes the pressure off both of you and gives you a chance to get to know each other.

Be prepared

Things do not always go as planned, so be prepared for rejection, just in case it happens. Your feelings may be hurt, and you may be angry at first, but there is no shame in being turned down. You just have to chalk it up to experience and be glad that you at least had the guts to give it a try.

Rejection is never easy. You can reduce your chances of being told no by asking out only people who have already given you signals that they like you, too.

50

Love and affection

Once you start dating, you should do only what you feel comfortable with and no more. When you care about someone, there are lots of ways to show your affection. Holding hands, cuddling and kissing each other are great ways to show your feelings if these are things you both want to do and feel ready for.

When you have been going steady with someone for a while, one of you may want to do more. Petting is when you touch and stroke each other in a sexual way, for example stroking the breasts or penis. This can be exciting if you want to do it, but upsetting if you do not. The important thing is to say no when you think things are going too far, or to stop if you think your partner is unhappy. You should never have sex or do things you do not want just to make a boy- or girl-friend like you more, or because you think they will dump you if you don't. Your body is your own.

Lots of people worry that they are going to be bad kissers. If you simply relax and do what comes naturally, it will be fine.

TOP TIPS

If you decide your relationship is not working out, let your partner down gently. Keep in mind that you will both be happier in the long run.

● Be clear about why you want to split up. Being direct will save a lot of time and stress.
● Try not to be cruel. Don't make it a personal attack, and try to be sensitive.
● Pick the place. Meet alone somewhere away from school and other friends.
● Pick the right time. Don't dump someone the day before an important exam or on their birthday.

Learn to love yourself

With so many changes and challenges happening to you during puberty, it's hardly surprising that most people feel self-conscious about the way they look or behave. Some people end up comparing themselves to others and become convinced that they don't match up. You need to develop self-esteem, or self-confidence, to become your own person. If you know and respect yourself, you can make the choices that are right for you.

Build it up

Building up your confidence is a bit like building up your muscles—you need to work at it on a regular basis. One thing you can do is to think and be more positive about yourself. For example, instead of worrying about what you cannot do or do not like, focus on the things you do well or that you like about yourself. If there are things you dislike but can't change, like your height, focus on the good things, like the fact you have nice eyes or great hair. Some people find it boosts their confidence to join a new class or learn a new skill. It can be tough to take the first step, but you might be surprised how good this can make you feel about yourself.

Being positive about yourself is the key to changing your self-image and your whole life!

CHECK IT OUT

Self-harming is when people hurt themselves regularly in some way, such as cutting or burning themselves. It affects some people during puberty, when they feel their intense emotions are out of control. Self-harming is dangerous and people who do it risk injuring themselves permanently. It is also a sign that a person needs help dealing with their emotions, so if you or someone you know does this, get help as soon as possible.

You ARE beautiful!!

Me too!

It will be a chance to make new friends, too. Sometimes, a simple thing, such as altering your body language, can make you feel and look more confident. Practice holding your head up high, walking tall and looking people in the eyes, and you will see and feel a difference.

TOP TIP

Remember that everyone has things they don't like about themselves, even if they seem to be super cool and confident on the outside. Don't sit in a corner comparing yourself to other people—get out there and enjoy yourself instead.

Quiz

How good are you at handling the relationships in your life? (Answers on page 61)

1. Your parents refuse to let you go to a party. Do you

a) talk it over with them and try to work out a compromise?

b) scream and shout at them?

c) go anyway, but lie to them by saying you are staying at a friend's house?

2. Your best friend says she or he is spending the weekend with another friend. Do you

a) make plans to do something else, happy in the knowledge you are best friends, even if you see other friends sometimes, too?

b) go to his or her house anyway and insist they let you join them?

c) ignore him or her for a week?

3. When you are upset, a friend would

a) ask you what is wrong and encourage you to talk about it.

b) leave you alone. When you're in a mood, you're no fun to be around.

c) suggest you talk to a parent or teacher about it.

4. Are you too obsessed with that special someone?

a) You think about them a lot, but you are as busy as ever.

b) Your school books have hearts and his or her initials all over them.

c) You have lost your appetite, you are way behind with your homework and your friends are sick of hearing about it.

53

Staying healthy

Your body is going through a lot of changes right now so it is important to look after it. You may think you have too much going on in your life to think about things such as what you eat and how often to shower, but you have just one body, so you need to treat it right!

Try to find a healthy balance when choosing what to eat.

Eat up

Eating a balanced diet is important throughout your life, but especially during puberty. Your body needs good food to fuel its rapid growth. Eating well will also help you to look good. A balanced diet means plenty of carbohydrates, fruit and vegetables, milk and dairy foods, enough protein and small amounts of fats and sugars. Drink plenty of water, too. Water keeps you healthy, helps you concentrate and helps keep your skin looking good.

If you eat healthily and exercise, you should not have a weight problem. If you do decide to diet, do it properly. You should ask a doctor for advice before you start any diet. The healthiest and best way to lose a few pounds is simply to eat smaller portions, fewer fatty foods and more fruit and vegetables. Getting into new eating habits like this will mean that once you lose the weight, you will not put it on again.

CHECK IT OUT

Eating disorders can be very dangerous and cause permanent damage to your body. They can affect both boys and girls. Bulimia is when people eat large amounts of food and then force themselves to throw it up to keep from putting on weight. Anorexia is when people starve themselves in an attempt to lose weight. If you have a problem like this, get help from a parent or other adult, and see your doctor as soon as possible.

54

Get up and get out!

Regular exercise keeps you fit and at a healthy weight, and it also boosts your body in other ways at this crucial time. For one thing, exercise relieves stress because it makes your body produce endorphins, chemicals that help you feel happier and more positive. If you care about the way you look, exercise also helps your appearance. It gives you a toned body and a healthy glow. Exercise can also help you sleep better so that you have more energy during the day.

Most teenagers need between 7 and 10 hours of sleep each night. Often a catnap will help keep you feeling perky.

Sleep in

You need plenty of sleep during puberty because the hormone that causes your growth spurt is released while you are sleeping. Chances are you get far less sleep than you need, and this can lead to moodiness, lack of concentration, and depression. The problem partly comes down to hormones. In teenagers the sleep-control hormone, melatonin, tends to kick in later in the day than it does in adults, so you may not feel tired when it's time to go to bed. You can try to catch up on your sleep on the weekend, but it's better to find ways of getting to sleep earlier in the week. Try taking a bath, drinking warm milk, or reading for half an hour before turning the lights out.

Taking care of yourself

It's one of the cruel ironies of life that you may start to get pimples and sweat more just at the time you become most self-conscious about the way you look. You can't really avoid these problems, but you can do things that help.

Why do you get pimples?

Pimples are caused by an oily substance in the skin called sebum. Your body produces sebum to keep your skin soft, supple and waterproof. During puberty your body produces more sebum, some of which can block the tiny pores (holes) in your skin. These blocked holes trap bacteria, which then multiply and form pimples. Most people get pimples on the face, but they can also appear on the neck, upper back, shoulders, and chest.

The good news about pimples is that you can treat them in a number of ways, from antibacterial soaps to face masks.

Try to resist the temptation to squeeze pimples. This may leave you with scars, and if your fingers are dirty it can cause an infection. Instead wash your face gently with soap or cleanser every day and pat it dry with a clean towel.

CHECK IT OUT

Eight out of ten teenagers suffer from pimples in some way, whether they get the odd pimple or suffer from acne. Girls often find their pimples are worse around the time of their period, while boys may have a more constant problem.

Don't scrub your face too hard as this can encourage your skin to produce even more oils. If you get a pimple, dab it with a pimple treatment stick. This should get rid of it after about two days. If you have a bigger problem with pimples, try an antibacterial face wash for a couple of weeks. If your acne is very severe, then you should see your doctor for another form of treatment.

Get into a regular routine of keeping your skin, teeth, hair and body clean and you might not be the only one to notice the improvement!

TOP TIP

The extra sebum your skin produces during puberty can also cause greasy hair. To keep greasy hair clean, wash it often with a mild shampoo. (It's not true that washing your hair every day makes it greasy.) If you use conditioner, make sure it is oil-free and designed for greasy hair. If you use a hair dryer, don't use it on the hottest setting because the heat will encourage your scalp to produce more oil.

Banish BO

Now is the time to make showers a part of your daily routine. The reason body odor (BO) suddenly becomes an issue during puberty is that you start to sweat in a different way. You have two kinds of sweat glands and one, called the apocrine glands, starts working only at puberty. Although the sweat these glands produce has no smell itself, when normal skin bacteria decompose it, it starts to .stink. As well as regular washing, you should change your clothes, underwear and socks every day and use deodorant or antiperspirant to make your armpits smell nice.

57

Dos and don'ts

In addition to knowing the things to do to look after yourself, you also need to know what *not* to do! This includes smoking, drinking alcohol and taking drugs.

Smoking

Smoking is definitely one thing your body can do without. And even if the very serious risk of getting cancer from long-term smoking seems too far into the future to think about, but what about the immediate effects? Cigarette smoking will cost you a lot of money. Smoking also makes your clothes and hair smell, stains your fingers, gives you bad breath, makes you cough, and dries out your skin.

The last thing smoking does is make you more attractive to the opposite sex.

Drinking and drugs

Alcohol and drugs change the way your body works. They react with your brain to alter your sense of reality, your emotions, movement, sight, speech and hearing. Taking harmful substances like this, while your body is still growing and developing, can have serious consequences. For example, alcohol slows down your body processes, and if you drink too much in a short period of time, they can slow down so much that you become unconscious and even die.

CHECK IT OUT

People who drink alcohol or take drugs at parties run the risk of doing something they may deeply regret later. Alcohol and drugs make you confused, and you may take risks like getting into a car with a drunk driver or having sex with someone you do not know or like. Remember, it is possible to get pregnant or to catch an STI from just one act of unprotected sex.

Becoming addicted

The real problem with cigarettes, alcohol, and drugs is that they are addictive. That means they contain chemicals that make you dependent on them so that after a while you want more and more. Studies have shown that the earlier you start smoking or drinking alcohol, the greater the risk you will become addicted. This is great for the people who make and sell these things, but not for you. Addiction can literally ruin peoples' lives, affecting their work, relationships and health. You owe it to yourself to respect your body and value your future, so don't let anything get in the way of that.

Growing up can be quite a challenge sometimes, but it's also one of the most exciting and exhilarating times of your life, so make the most of it!

The last word…

Even after reading this book you may still have questions you want answered. There may be things that you find hard to talk about with your parents, and getting answers from your friends is not always the best solution because they may not have all the correct information, however confident they seem. At the end of this book is a list of telephone numbers and websites where you can get more facts and advice. You could also talk to your doctor, a school nurse, teacher, school counselor, or other adults who you feel comfortable talking to. The important thing is not to waste too much of your time worrying about things—get the answers or advice you need to feel confident and relaxed, and then get out there and enjoy yourself.

Questions and answers

Why am I hungry all the time?
You're probably hungry because, during puberty, your body needs food to fuel growth. Many people worry this will lead to them getting fat, but it won't as long as you don't use your cravings as an excuse to eat junk food. Instead of snacking on chocolate or chips, reach for cereal bars, bananas, apples, or bags of trail mix when you get hunger pangs, and eat plenty of filling, but healthy, whole-grain carbohydrates, such as brown rice and pasta, at main meals.

What can I do about my pimples?
Picking or squeezing is not an option—this just makes the area red and sore and may leave you with a scar. Treat pimples with a dab-on spot treatment and, if you like, hide them with a cover-up product until they go away. Don't scrub too harshly; simply wash your skin gently with a mild cleanser and use an oil-free moisturizer. For more serious acne, a doctor should be able to prescribe something.

Why do I smell all of a sudden?
If sweat is left on your skin, bacteria break it down, releasing chemicals that make a nasty smell. During puberty, hormones in sweat glands in the armpits and genital areas start to become active, and bacteria particularly like to feed on sweat there. The only solution is to take regular showers, wear clean clothes and use deodorants or antiperspirants.

Who can I talk to about getting contraception?
You can make an appointment with your doctor to find out more about contraception. This is usually confidential but check with the office about its confidentiality policy. If you feel uncomfortable talking to your doctor, see if there's a family planning clinic in your area. And remember your parents are always there to answer your questions and guide you throughout puberty and the years beyond.

Will I still be a virgin if I use tampons?
Yes. Only having sexual intercourse makes you lose your virginity. Some people think a broken hymen is a sign a girl is not a virgin. In fact, most teenage girls use smaller tampons, which do not usually damage the hymen.

Help! I think I have an STI.
The problem with STIs is that the symptoms are hard to spot and you may not even notice them. The only way to be sure is to see a doctor.

Are my periods too heavy?
A normal amount of blood loss each period is between 4 and 12 teaspoonfuls, but every girl or woman loses different amounts and types of blood during a period. Some women lose a small amount of thin, dark blood; others might lose more and it might be bright red. Sometimes you might pass lumpy blood clots too, or you might see small flakes in with the menstrual blood. All of this is normal, but if you're worried, you can see your doctor just to be sure.

What can I do about my greasy hair?
Wash regularly with a shampoo designed for greasy hair, and always wash hair after exercising to prevent sweat oils from building up on your scalp. Try not to touch your hair too much as this encourages the glands to produce extra oil. One mistake people make is to wear a hat all the time to cover the hair—this just stops sweat on the scalp from evaporating and makes matters worse.

Why are my PJs wet when I wake up?

This is because you have had what is known as a wet dream. A wet dream is when a boy ejaculates during his sleep, usually while he is having a dream that has sexual images. You can't control wet dreams or stop them from happening. Just keep tissues by your bed to clean up any mess and save any embarrassment by changing your own bed sheets.

Why am I always arguing with my parents?

It's natural for teens and parents to argue, but it can get out of hand. Although it's hard, try not to lose your temper. Try to argue fairly without interrupting other people. Avoid insults and argue respectfully and only when there is something important to argue about—try not to fall into the habit of arguing about everything. Try to reach compromises when you can and you are more likely to earn each other's respect and trust.

Is my penis too small?

Everyone goes through puberty at different rates so do not compare yourself to other boys. Anyway, in most cases the penis doesn't stop growing till you are between 18 and 21. Boys often worry because the testicles grow earlier than the penis, and that makes them think their penis is too small. Also, if you're a bit overweight, fat tissue slightly hides the penis and makes it look smaller than it really is.

How do I stop obsessing about my crush?

It's OK to have some time alone fantasizing about your crush, but it should not be taking over your life. Find a hobby that will get you out of the house and meeting new people. Catch up on your schoolwork and ask your friends to distract you.

How do you know when you are ready for sex?

Well, until you reach the age of consent in your state, it is against the law to have sex. Even then, it is hard to be sure when the time is right, and most teens choose to wait. Having sex for the first time is a big step, and it can affect your physical and emotional health. Remember, too, that no contraceptive is 100 percent reliable. Have you really thought about what you would do if faced with an unplanned pregnancy?

Quiz Answers

Page 9

1. (a); 2. (a); 3. (a); 4. (a); 5. (a).
If you answered all "a"s, then you can go to the head of the class!

Page 21

1. True
2. True
3. True
4. True
5. False—you should dispose of them in a wastebasket.
6. False—it stands for premenstrual syndrome.
7. True
8. False—shaving makes hair grow back thicker and darker.

Page 31

1. (a); 2. (b); 3. (b); 4. b); 5. (b); 6. (b).
All "b"s means you were paying attention.

Page 41

1. False
2. True
3. False—there is always a risk of pregnancy even when people use contraception.
4. False—ECP stands for emergency contraceptive pill.
5. True
6. False—it is never safe to meet up with someone you know only through the Internet.

Page 53

1. The best option is "a" because the other choices cause strife with your parents.
2. Again, the best choice is "a." If you chose one of the other options, you are getting too possessive of your friend.
3. A good friend would choose "a," although they might also be right to suggest you talk to a parent or teacher if they thought it was something they could not help with.
4. If your crush leaves you feeling like "a," you are OK, but if you chose "b" or "c" you're in danger of letting your crush take over your life.

Glossary

acne a common skin disease among teenagers in which oil and hair glands become inflamed and cause pimples (whiteheads) and blackheads

addiction when someone becomes so dependent on something, for example a drug, that he or she feels they cannot do without it

age of consent the age that a person is legally believed to be mature enough to choose to have sexual intercourse

anorexia the condition, or disorder, in which people starve themselves in an attempt to lose weight for so long that they lose their appetite completely

bacterial relating to or caused by bacteria. Bacteria are microscopic one-celled organisms, some of which are essential for our survival while others cause disease

bulimia a condition, or disorder, in which a person goes through phases of eating large amounts of food at one sitting and then gets rid of it by vomiting or using laxatives, so that the food does not make them put on weight

carbohydrates sugars and starches found in breads, cereals, fruits and vegetables that give us energy when we eat them

condom a form of contraception that consists of a sheath (or sock) of thin rubber or latex that men wear over their penis during sexual intercourse

confidential when something is confidential it is private and should not be repeated to anyone else

contraception a method used to prevent pregnancy when a couple have sexual intercourse

eating disorders serious problems with eating that can damage a person's health

ejaculation the release of semen from the penis

emergency contraceptive pill (EPC) a tablet that a woman can take up to three days after having sex to prevent pregnancy

endorphins the group of chemicals produced in the brain that reduce pain and improve your mood

erection when the blood supply to blood vessels in the penis increases, usually after a boy or man becomes sexually excited, and his penis becomes bigger and rigid

family planning center where people go for medical advice about contraception or planning a family

fertilization what happens when a male sperm cell joins with a female ovum, or egg cell. The fertilized egg cell grows into a baby

foreplay sexual activity such as caressing, touching, stroking and kissing that people do before having sexual intercourse

genetic caused by genes. Genes are a kind of code that makes us the way we are. They are passed from parent to child at conception

genitals the external sex organs such as the vagina and penis

glands organs that make and release one or more substances needed by the body, such as growth hormones that tell your body when to grow

homosexuality when a person is sexually attracted to someone who is the same sex as them

hymen the thin sheet of skin tissue that partly covers the lower end of the entrance to the vagina

inter-uterine inside the uterus, or womb

lubricate to make something slippery or smooth by smearing it with a lubricant, such as a cream or oil

masturbation when a person touches his or her own genitals to get sexual pleasure

menopause the time in a woman's life in which her menstrual cycle comes to an end

menstrual cycle the time between one of a woman's periods and the next, usually about 28 days

orgasm the peak of sexual pleasure that both men and women experience

ova female sex cells, also known as eggs or egg cells

ovaries the female reproductive organs that produce eggs and female sex hormones

ovum singular of ova. *See* ova

painkiller medicine used to relieve pain

premenstrual syndrome (PMS) a variety of symptoms some girls and women experience for several days before their periods start each month, such as irritability, tearfulness and changes in mood

pubic area the area on and around the genitals, which is usually covered in pubic hair after puberty

puberty the physical changes that happen to a child's body to turn it into an adult body capable of reproduction

reproduce when a male and a female conceive and have babies

sebum an oily substance made and released by glands in the skin

self-esteem the feeling of being pleased with, proud or confident with oneself

sexual abuse when someone forces another person to have sex or do anything sexual with them that the other person does not want to do

sexually transmitted infection (STI) an infection or disease passed on by sexual contact

spotting when a girl or woman loses a little bit of blood toward the end of her period

straight to be heterosexual, or attracted to people of the opposite sex

testes plural of testis, an alternative name for testicle. *See* testicle

testicle the egg-shaped gland found inside the male scrotum. Testes produce sperm and male hormones

testosterone the male sex hormone that is produced in the testes or testicles

---

Web sites and associations

There are a number of organizations that can help if you need more advice or information.

Teen Growth A resource web site for teens; covering all topics from sports to sexual health and the changing body. **www.teengrowth.com/**

Teens Health A database of different articles and facts about teens' changing bodies, information about STDs, and more. **www.kidshealth.org/teen/sexual_health/**

I Wanna Know A web site developed by the American Social Health Association to educate teenagers on sexually transmitted infections. **www.iwannaknow.org**

KidsHealth This web site has lots of information and links about puberty and other teen issues. Visit **http://kidshealth.org/kid/grow/body_stuff/puberty.html**

Planned Parenthood The largest sexual and reproductive health care provider in the United States, which offers a variety of health services and counseling. **www.plannedparenthood.com**

Gay-Straight Alliance Network A youth leadership organization dedicated to fighting discrimination, educating school communities about homophobia, sexual orientation, and gender identity. Helps students start and maintain these clubs in different schools. **www.gsanetwork.org**

Child Help Free 24-hour confidential helpline dedicated to the prevention of child abuse. All calls are anonymous and come from children who are abused, parents, and people who suspect abuse. The helpline is 1-800-422-4453 or visit **www.childhelp.org**

National Eating Disorders Association An organization that provides education, support, and resources for people who suffer from eating disorders. Their helpline is 800-931-2237. **www.nationaleatingdisorders.org**

Sex, Etc. A web site and organization that strives to help improve teen sexual health in the United States through education. **www.sexetc.org**

Index

Numbers in **BOLD** refer to illustrations